GIANFRANC...

guide to the
PANTHEON

EDITORIALE MUSEUM

© *Copyright* 1990 Editoriale Museum S.r.l. Roma

Photographs: Luciano Pedicini

Illustrations: Soprintendenza Beni Ambientali e Architettonici di Roma
                                                          Hertzian Library

Lay-out: Sabrina Moroni

Production and printing: ATS Italia - Roma

V° Reprint: March 1995

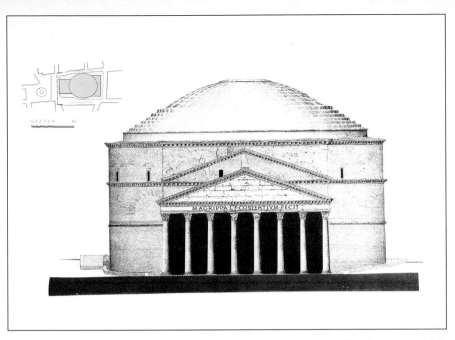

1. *Facade of the Pantheon, Soprintendenza ai Beni Ambientali e Architettonici di Roma*

HISTORY

The search for the sacred place, set apart from daily use and dedicated to the gods, where mankind could establish and renew its mutual pact with the divine, was a constant feature of the ancient world. In the city of Rome one of the most significant of these places was that delimited by the area where two small streams met, Aqua Sallustiana and the Annis Petronia.

The geology and topography of the site had led to the formation of a large swampy area situated beween the Quirinal and Capitol hills and the left bank of the Tiber.

Tradition held that in the centre of this area, the Palus Caprae, the mythical founder of Rome was transformed into a hero and carried off into the heavens by Mars. A tumulus was probably erected to record the event and subsequently, in the augustan period, influenced by fashionable ideas favouring a return to tradition, a temple was built on the site in 27 B.C. by Marcus Agrippa. The building was rectangular and the entrance was placed in the southern facade following the Etruscan custom for burial.

After having suffered from two fires the temple was rebuilt from the ground up in 120 A.D. by the emperor Hadrian who inverted the previous

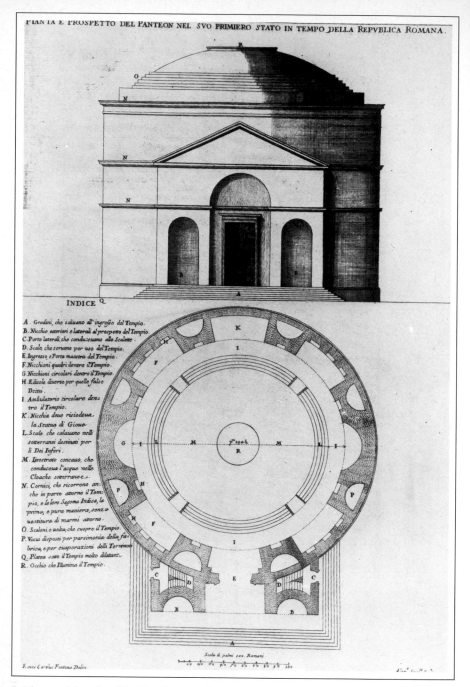

2. *Plan and facade of the Pantheon in the period of the Republic (C. Fontana, Rome, 1694)*

3. The entrance: original bronze doors of the Augustan period

orientation and had fixed to the entablature of the portico the inscription in bronze letters of the original founder: M. AGRIPPA L. F. COS. TERTIUM. FECIT (Erected by Marcus Agrippa, son of Lucio, for the third time consul). The dedication of the temple to all the gods, resumed in the name "Pantheon", could on the other hand, according to an authoritative interpretation, derive from a dedication to one single god, Nature. The temple complex consisted of a large colonnaded square and an entrance portico approached by six steps which formed the compositional link to the great hall itself.

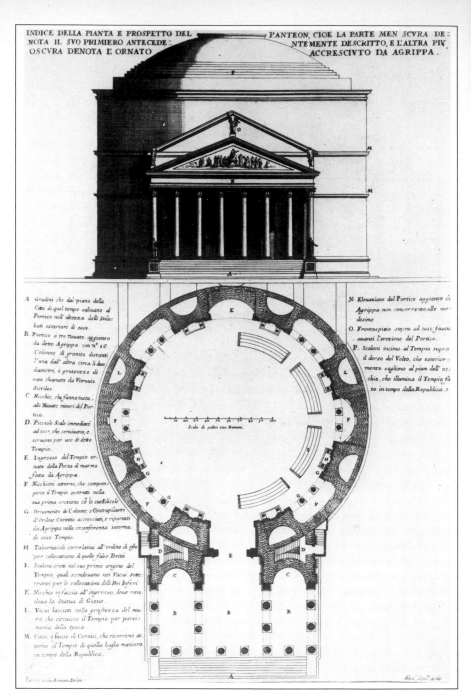

4. Plan and facade of the Pantheon of Agrippa (C. Fontana, Rome 1694)

5. *Rome, Piazza della Rotonda*

The entrance portico is formed by sixteen columns set up in three rows, eight of the columns in gray-green, and the rest in pink granite. Of the seven spacings between the eight columns of the facade the central one is perfectly aligned with the entrance.

If the pediment of the portico is projected geometrically into the rear pediment they are found to coincide, providing a further proof that the building was designed and realized as a single unit.

The great hall, which is entered through the original bronze door mounted on a sill of African green marble, is based on the form of a sphere - that most perfect of all the geometrical possibilities - and has two openings, one on the horizontal and one on the vertical axis.

The upper half of the sphere makes up the cupola of the roof and is divided into twentyeight vertical slices, each divided again into five horizontal courses, plus a sixth which is taken up by the opening in the cupola.

The lower half below the cupola is divided again into an upper part which originally contained sixty four panels of polychrome marble framed in porphyry, plus the lower part consisting of three

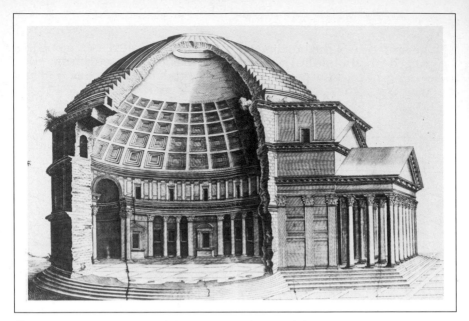

6. *Section of the Pantheon (Blaeu, Amsterdam, 1704)*

semicircular niches, the entrance, four rectangular niches and eight tabernacles mounted on the structural pillars of the cupola.

Sunlight, defined in the classical past as the "great regulator" had been commonly used with sundials and obelisks to fix during equinoxes the orientation of given sites, and generally as a time teller; in the case of the Pantheon a revolution occurs: sunlight, falling on the interior of the structure, indicates precisely not only the dates of the equinoxes and solstices but also the passing of the hours.

For this reason an area corresponding with the present position of the great altar remains always in the shade while from the entrance it is possible to see the sun at noon.

Between the summer solstice (the lowest point) and the winter solstice (the highest point) the area of the equinoxes coincides with the horizontal strip between the attic storey and the first course of ceiling coffers. This play of sunlight probably served to establish a calendar for the three-part holy year and four-part normal year by means of a set of signs and symbols marked on the coffers.

Organized in this way the building conforms to laws of proportion which in the case of the Pantheon are established on a one-to-two basis, a "divine proportion" which leads to the overall harmony of the architectural expression.

The structure of the building is based on the skilful use of relieving arches, above all in in the masonry of the cylinder which supports the cupola.

The entire load is taken on a continuous ring of concrete, mixed with travertine fragments, protected by a facing of semilateres, 7.30 metres wide, 4.5 metres high.

The foundations, as a remedy for settlement along the north-south axis, were reinforced by additional tracts of foundation laid parallel to the original, and by the construction of buttresses along the failure line of the settlement.

Up to the first cornice to a height of 12.5 metres the masonry cylinder carrying the cupola is built of a nucleus of alternating strata of travertine and tufo faced with semilateres. At regular intervals of 1.2 metres are inserted courses of bipedali. These courses confirm the notion of a "working day", a number of hours which gave the masonry time in which to set.

From the first cornice up to the springing of the cupola, for a height of 9.5 metres, the masonry is

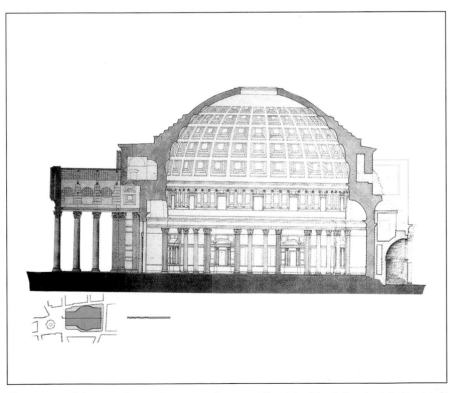

7. Section of the Pantheon, Soprintendenza ai Beni Ambientali e Architettonici di Roma

8. *The Pantheon and builder Agrippa (F. de' Ficoroni, Rome, 1744)*

made up of alternate strata of tufo and brick fragments, set in a mortar bed, faced with semilateres and built with courses of bipedali at intervals of 1.2 metres.

The cupola, constructed on semispherical shuttering, is built from the springing up to a height of 11.75 metres of small brick fragments and courses of bipedali laid at varying intervals. For a further height of 2.25 metres the masonry is composed of tufo, brick fragments and close-laid courses of bipedali.

Up to the ring of the opening there is further use of tufo and volcanic matter while the ring itself, approximately 9 metres in diameter, is constructed in concentric rings of bipedali 1.40 metres thick.

The exterior of the vault is faced in semilateres laid in a herring-bone pattern and covered with a layer of opus signinum on which was laid the original outer roof surface of gilded bronze tiles.

9. The cupola seen from the interior

10. *The Pantheon during Emperor Constantine's reign (200 A.D.) - (Rome, Museo della Civiltà Romana, detail of plastic)*

CHANGE AND RESTORATIONS

T he monument has had a che-quered history. Septimus Severus and Caracalla were responsible for a restoration in 202 A.D., mounting an additional inscription below the original which read
IMP. CAES. L. SEPTIMIUS SEVERUS... ET IMP. M. AURELIUS ANTONINUS... PANTHEUM VETUSTATE CORRUPTUM CUM OMNI CULTU RESTITUERUNT (The emperor L. Septimus Severus and the emperor M. Aurelius Antoninus... carefully restored the Pantheon, ruined by the passage of the years). In 608 the Pantheon was conceded by the emperor Foca to pope Boniface IV who transfor-med it into a church dedicated to S. Maria ad Martyres.

Fifty years later the cupola was stripped of its roof of bronze tiles by the emperor Costant II; in 735 pope Gregorius III had it reclad with lead sheeting which although saving it from ruin was no contri-bution to its look or quality, given especially the difference in the capacity of the two metals with respect to their relationship with the underlying structure.

Throughout the Middle Ages the Pantheon found itself at the centre

11. The Pantheon with the central belfry of the thirteenth century (A. Donati, Rome, 1665)

of the struggles between the various factions of Rome who contended control of the city.

Pope Anastasius IV (1153-54) initiated the construction of a building next to the Pantheon designed to house the papal canons which was completed by his successor Hadrian IV (1154-59). Callisto III ceded the possession of the piazza to the canons who were thus entitled to taxes levied on the merchants who used the space. (This usage was confirmed by his successors up to Urban VIII).

Urban VIII (1623-1644) stripped the beams of the building of their bronze cladding, replaced the first column on the left of the portico and had the belfry built on top of the pediment of the portico demolished and substituted with two bell towers set on the top of the second internal pediment, designed by

12. "The emperor Foca donating the Pantheon to Pope Boniface IV" (Oil on canvas, 1750)

Gian Lorenzo Bernini.

Alexander VII (1657-67), with the help of Giuseppe Paglia, replaced

13. The Pantheon with the twin steeples designed by Bernini (Marchi, watercolour on paper, Rome, 1754).

14. *Pope Boniface IV. Bronze portrait bust by F. Sansone, (1990)*

two other columns on the left-hand side of the portico using those in red granite which had been found in the Alexandrine Baths near S. Luigi dei Francesi. The pope had the level of the piazza lowered and ordered the demolition of a number of houses belonging to the Capitolo in order to undertake excavations along the side of the portico which, in order to avoid its occupation by the merchants of the piazza, he had enclosed with a railing. Among the restorations undertaken by his successors figure that of Innocent XI (1676-89) who had the roof of the cupola repaired, and that of Clement XI (1700-21) who rebuilt the great altar and its apse, as well as adding to the fountain in the

15. *Detail of the portico. On the left the three columns in pink granite which replaced the destroyed originals in the seventeenth century*

16. The portico with the original railing (Rome, 1818)

piazza an obelisk found at S. Macuto.

In 1747 Paolo Posi, under the orders of Benedict XIV (1740-58) who had withdrawn the monument from the jurisdition of the Roman senate and entrusted its maintenance and care to the office of the apostolic palaces, substituted (in an operation whose significance has still to be investigated and explained) the original cladding of the attic storey with 14 blind windows alternated with framed squares. An area of the attic was partially restored in 1930 by the architect Alberto Terenzio, who based the restoration on drawings by Raffaello Sanzio and Baldassare Peruzzi. During the Napoleonic period the French government prepared a project for the enlargement of the piazza while Pius VII (1800-

23) launched a general cleaning-up operation which included the demolition of buildings attached to the monument. He also brought to an end a usage established in 1766 which had consisted of putting up memorial portrait busts in the building, transferring the entire collection to the Protomoteca Capitolina which he had founded in 1820.

The cleaning-up of the Pantheon and its immediate area was continued by Pius IX in 1857 and subsequently by the Italian government itself. On the death of Victor Emanuel II (9 January 1878) King Umberto I, in an informal personal decision, decided that the burial should take place in the Pantheon rather than in the palace of Superga. The same decision was taken by Victor Emanuel III, regarding Umberto I and, subsequently,

17. The Piazza of the Pantheon, fountain with the obelisk

his mother, Margaret of Savoy.
The National Institute of Honour Guards to the Royal Tombs, founded in 1878, is responsible of the organizing the pickets. The building has now been entrusted to the care of the Soprintendenza per i Beni Ambientali e Architettonici del Lazio and is the object of careful maintenance and continuous and indispensable restoration. The present look of the building is still, essentially, that of the original: from the floor laid in precious marble (porphyry, pavonazzetto, giallo antico and granite), restored by Pius IX in 1873, to the lower storey articulated by rectangular and semicircular niches faced with fluted columns in giallo antico, linked by the great structural columns which hold up the cupola on which are set eight tabernacles trimmed with columns of granite, porphyry and giallo antico, crowned by alter-

nate triangular and semicircular pediments, to the attic storey faced today with blank window and stuccoed frames, to the overhanging cupola itself.
The Feasts of the Ascension and Assumption were celebrated in the church with particular solemnity. On these occasions a sacred representation took place in which the statues of Christ and the Virgin were drawn up until they disappeared in the cupola, and at Pentecost rose-petals were dropped down from above. On the fourth Sunday of Pentecost the Pope blessed the golden roses which were to be sent to those Christian kings who had merited them. And finally, for the Feast of S. Giuseppe di Terrasanta, a group of artists associated with the Congregazione dei Virtuosi exposed their works in the portico.

18. Left-hand side of the portico with the door of the Congregazione dei Virtuosi

PLAN OF THE PANTHEON

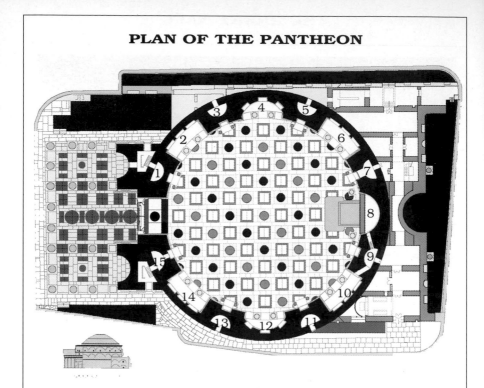

1) **First tabernacle**

2) **First chapel**
   The Chapel of the Virtuosi

3) **Second tabernacle**

4) **Second chapel**
   Tombs of Umberto I and
   Margherita of Savoy

5) **Third tabernacle**

6) **Third chapel**
   Chapel of the Crucifixion

7) **Fourth tabernacle**

8) **Fourth caphel**

9) **Fifth tabernacle**

10) **Fifth chapel**

11) **Sixth tabernacle**

12) **Sixth chapel**
    Tomb of
    Vittorio Emanuele II

13) **Seventh tabernacle**

14) **Seventh chapel**

15) **Eighth tabernacle**

19. The interior of the great hall looking towards the great altar

T he present arrangement of the paintings, sculpture and inscriptions in the tabernacles and chapels is the result of numerous changes and transformations which do not seem to be the result of a well-defined program. Some of these works whose memory is preserved in the older texts are no longer to be found, and the original dedications of the various chapels are uncertain although recent studies may provide a clarification which could lead to a definitive arrangement of the furnishings.

Before beginning the tour of the hall one should observe the series of niches-practically all empty-placed at the sides of the tabernacles which were prepared to house the portrait busts of the Virtuosi, removed subsequently by Pius VII. The description of the furnishings runs clockwise around the hall:

1) First tabernacle on the left.
Assumption, by Andrea Camassei, oil on canvas, 1638.

2) First chapel on the left.

20. The first tabernacle and the Cappella dei Virtuosi

The Chapel of the Virtuosi.
This famous and illustrious institution was founded by Canon Desiderio da Segni who, on his return from a pilgrimage to the Holy Land, received the chapel, at that time in a state of abandon, in donation from the Capitolo.
Once restored he dedicated it to S. Giuseppe and had a casket placed on the floor containing soil from Palestine collected during his voyage. To guarantee support for the cult of the chapel he founded an association which was confirmed as a confraternity by Paul III in 1543.
Amongst the first members of the Confraternity, made up of painters, sculptors and architects, are to be found, amongst others, Antonio da Sangallo the younger, Jacopo Meneghino, Giovanni Mangone, Taddeo Zuccari, Domenico Beccafumi and Flaminio Vacca.
Subsequent members included Caravaggio, Gian Lorenzo Bernini, Pietro da Cortona, Alessandro Algardi, Claude Lorrain, Vignola, Maderno, Vanvitelli, Valadier, Canina, Batoni, Canova, Camuccini and many others.
The institution continues to exist today as the Accademia Pontificia di Belle Arti, with its seat in the palace of the Cancelleria.
On the altar of the chapel lined with artificial marble: *S. Giuseppe and the Child Jesus*, sculpture by Vincenzo De Rossi (1525-87), at the sides of which are two paintings by Franceco Cozza (a Virtuoso), *The Adoration of the Shepherds* (on the left) and *the Adoration of the Magi* (on the right), dated 1661.
On the side walls two stucco reliefs depicting the *Dream of S. Giuseppe*, by Paolo Benaglia (on the left) and *Rest during the flight from Egypt*, by Carlo Monaldi (on the right).
On the vault, from left to right, seventeenth century paintings on canvas:

21. The second tabernacle. Bust of Baldassare Peruzzi, statue of Saint Agnes (V. Felici, seventeenth century)

The Cuman Sibyl, by Ludovico Gemignani: Moses, by Francesco Rosa; *The Eternal Father*, by Giovanni Peruzzini; *David*, by Luigi Garzi; *The Eritrean Sibyl*, by Giovanni Andrea Carloni.
Numerous commemorative inscriptions of the Virtuosi are also to be found in the Chapel.

3) Second tabernacle.
S. Agnes, sculpture by Vincenzo Felici, an artist active in Rome between the end of the seventeenth century and the beginning of the eighteenth. On the left a bust of *Baldassare Peruzzi*, derived from a plaster likeness by Giovanni Dupré, and a commemorative inscription of the artist.

4) Second chapel.
This chapel, previously dedicated to S. Michele Arcangelo and subse-

22. The interior with the tombs of Umberto I and Margaret of Savoy

quently to S. Tommaso, was totally transformed to house the tombs of Umberto I and Margaret of Savoy by Giuseppe Sacconi who based the design on his previous project

23. The third tabernacle. The Tomb of Raphael

for the monument to Victor Emanuel II, but by reason of the illness and death of the architect, the completion of the project was entrusted to his pupil Guido Cirilli. The tomb consists of a slab of alabaster mounted in a frame of gilded bronze surrounded by a frieze with allegorical representations of Generosity, by Eugenio Maccagnani, and Munificence, by Arnaldo Zocchi. In front of the tomb, an altar in porphyry with the royal arms, by Guido Cirilli.

5) Third tabernacle.
Madonna of the Stone, sculpture executed in 1523-24 by Lorenzo Lotto, known as Lorenzetto, with the help of Raffaello da Montelupo. The statue was commissioned by Raffaello Sanzio, who had chosen this as his burial place.

The tomb was opened in 1833 to verify whether it in fact contained the remains of the artist, which were transferred to a Roman sarcophagus donated by Pope Gregory XVI, and on which was transcribed an epigraph composed by Pietro Bembo the celebrated humanist: ILLE HIC EST RAPHAEL TIMUIT QUO SOSPITE VINCI/RERUM MAGNA PARENS ET MORIENTE MORI.
(Here lies Raphael, by whom [Nature] the mother of all things feared to be overcome whilst he was living, and, whilst he was dying, herself to die).
The present arrangement of the tomb was carried out in 1811 by Antonio Munoz.
The bust of the artist, on the left of the tabernacle, is by Giuseppe Fabris (1833). On the right of the

24. The Chapel of the Crucifix. Bust of Cardinal Consalvi by Bertle Thorwaldsen, (1824)

25. The third Chapel. Crucifix: Abore the altar, the fifteenth century wooden crucifix

26. The third tabernacle. "The Madonna of the stone", statue by Lorenzo Lotti, called Lorenzetto (1524)

27. The Chapel of the Canons. "Madonna of Saint Luke", painting of the fourteenth century

tabernacle two plaques: one in memory of Maria Bibiena, the other in commemoration of Annibale Carracci, with a dated inscription by Carlo Maratta.

6) Third chapel.
Of the Crucifixion.
The original Roman brick wall with three niches is still visible. On the altar: wooden *Crucifix*, fifteenth century. On the left-hand wall, *Descent of the Holy Ghost* oil

on canvas, by Pietro Labruzi, 1790.
On the right-hand wall: *Cardinal Consalvi presents to Pope Pius VII the five provinces restored to the Holy See*, a low relief in marble executed by the sculptor Bertel Thorwaldsen in 1824, and a bust of *Cardinal Agostino Rivarola*.

7) Fourth tabernacle.
S. Anastasio, sculpture by Francesco Moderati, 1717.

28. The great altar and the two lateral tabernacles

8) Fourth chapel.

The present great altar was designed by Alessandro Specchi (who was also responsible for the cross and the candelabrum in bronze) commissioned by Clement XI. There existed here previously a mediaeval ciborium with porphyry columns and the space immediately in front on the altar was closed off by a railing with pulpits. In the apse, a *Glory of all the Saints*, by Giovanni Guerra, 1544, and a majolica plaque *The Risen Virgin*, school of della Robbia, a copy of the Madonna of *S. Luca*, encaustic panel, placed in the Pantheon at the moment of its dedication to the Virgin, but almost certainly earlier in date. The original of this icon which is conserved in the Chapel of the Canons,

29. The sixth tabernacle.
"Saint Ann and the Virgin", statue by Lorenzo Ottoni called Lorenzone, (1648-1736)

30. The fifth chapel. "The Madonna of Mercy with Saint Francis and Saint John the Baptist" painting of the fifteenth century

30. The tomb of Victory Emanuel II

was crowned by the Vatican Capitolo the 8 september 1652.

The gold-ground mosaic placed in the apse vault dates from the period of Pope Albani, whose arms are to be found at the top of the two columns which frame the apse.

The wooden choir was built after a design of Luigi Poletti in 1840.

9) Fifth tabernacle.

S. Rasio, sculpture by Bernardino Cametti, 1725.

10) Fifth chapel.

On the altar: *The Madonna of Mercy between S. Francis and Saint John the Baptist*, painting of the Umbria/Lazio school of the fifteenth century.

The painting, originally hung in the large niche on the left-hand side of the portico where it was protected by a rail (hence the name, the Madonna of the Railing) was originally moved to the chapel of the Annunciation, and finally to its present position after 1837.

On the left-hand wall: a bronze epigram recording the restoration of the great altar by Clement XI.

On the right-hand wall: *The emperor Foca presenting the Pantheon to pope Boniface IV*, oil on canvas, 1750. On the floor of the chapel

32. Seventh chapel: The Annunciation", fresco by Melozzo da Forlì, fifteenth century

33. The ceiling of the seventh chapel (seventeenth century)

are to be noted, amongst others, three plaques with inscriptions: that of Marco Tebaldi (+ 1414), that of the jurist Paolo Pino Scocciapile (fifteenth century, previously placed in the floor of the portico), and finally that of a certain Gismonda (1476, in vulgar script).

11) Sixth tabernacle.

S. Anne and the Virgin, sculpture by Lorenzo Ottoni, called Il Lorenzone (1648-1736).

12) Sixth chapel, previously known as that of the Holy Ghost: its original character was altered to make room for the tomb of Victor Emanuel II. A competition was held to choose the executor of this work (in which Count Giuseppe Sacconi also participated) which was won by the architect Manfredo Manfredi whose final entry was approved on the 21 May 1885.
The tomb which was finished three years later consists of a

34. The eighth tabernacle: "The Madonna of the Girdle and Saint Nicholas of Bari", oil on canvas (1686)

35. *The seventh tabernacle. "The Incoronation of the Virgin", fifteenth century fresco*

large bronze plaque on which is written in commemoration VICTOR EMANUEL II FATHER OF THE COUNTRY surmounted by a bronze Roman eagle with below a shield with the arms of the house of Savoy resting on two palm fronds.

The marble cladding of the niche is the work of Francesco Prosperi and Francesco Benni, the sculpture that of Adolfo Laurenti.

At the centre above the tomb is hangs a golden lamp which burns in honour of Victor Emanuel III, who died in exile in Alexandria, Egypt in 1947.

13) Seventh tabernacle.
The Incoronation of the Virgin, fresco of the Tuscan school, fifteenth century.

14) Seventh chapel.
The baptismal font was originally placed here (the Pantheon having been a parish church from the tenth century until 1824, when

this function was suppressed). On the back wall, *The Annunciation*, a fresco attributed to Melozzo da Forlì, previously located in the second chapel on the left.
On the left: *S. Laurence and S. Agnes*, oil on canvas by Clemente Maioli (1645-50). On the right: *The Incredulity of Saint Thomas*, oil on canvas by Pietro Paolo Bonzi, called the Gobbo dei Carracci, 1633. On the side walls four bronze busts of the Canon Zuccarino (+1662), of the theologian and philospher Baldario (+1765) on the left, of Giacomo Gamba (nunzio in Spain) and of G. Albano Ghiberti (doctor of Leopold I) on the right.
Two marble angels are found here which were donated by Cardinal B. Tomasi to the Virtuosi in 1696, and subsequently by these to the Church Capitolo.

15) Eighth tabernacle.
The Madonna of the Girdle and S. Nicolas of Bari, oil on canvas, 1686.
After the Concordat of 1929 the Pantheon is constituled as the seat of the "military ordinary of the Italian state, on which depends the military Hospital (article 28, letter G) to which privileges were conceded similar to those enjoyed by the Palatine chapels.
At the present time the offices of the church are held by ecclesiastical canons.

GLOSSARY

Sun-dried or lightly-baked bricks are known as *lateres*.
Oven-baked bricks are called *lateres cocti* or *testae*.
The word *tegula* indicates an oven-baked brick of the type used typically on roofs.
The *tegula*, cut and ground, is also used as a normal structural brick.
The brick - obtained by hardening through baking once the air contained in the clay mixed with water is removed- can be considered as the first man-made component to be used in building.
The variety of oven-baked bricks is based on the module of the Roman brick which is 29.6cm.
For example:
The *bipedalis* is a square brick with a dimension of 2x29.6 = 59.2cm.

The *bessalis* is a square brick with a dimension of 1.5x29.6 = 44.4cm.
The *semilateres* is a triangular brick derived from halving the bessalis, with a dimension of 22.2cm.
Masonry works are structures built up of resistant material put together so as to form a continuous solid.
The natural and artifical materials are rendered cohesive by the addition of mortar.
Mortar is usally made up of three parts of pozzolana (ground tufaceous rock) and one of slaked lime; or of two parts of river sand and one of slaked lime.
To conclude: *opus signinum* is a conglomerate made up of brick fragments and brick dust, or of stone mixed with lime, of a pink colour, practically waterproof.

ESSENTIAL BIBLIOGRAPHY

Bartoccetti Vittorio, *Santa Maria ad martyres (Pantheon) (le chiese di Roma illustrate, 47)* Rome, 1960.

Beltrami Luca, *Il Pantheon rivendicato di Adriano*, Milan, 1929

Borsi Franco, Buscioni M.C. *Manfredo Manfredi e il classicismo della nuova Italia*, Milan, 1983.

Cerasoli Francesco, *I restauri del Pantheon dal sec.XV al sec XVIII*, "Bull.Com.", pp.280-289.

Choisy Auguste, *L'art de batir chez les Romains*, Parigi, 1873, ed it., Bologna, 1969.

Coarelli Filippo, *Il Pantheon, l'apoteosi di Augusto e l'apoteosi di Romolo*, "Anacleta Romana Istituti Danici", suppl X, 1983, pp. 41-46

Colini Antonio Maria-Gismondi Italo, *Contributi allo studio del Pantheon, La parete frontale dell'avancorpo e la data del portico*, "Bull Com." 44, 1926, pp.67 sg.

De Fine Licht K,*The Rutunda in Rome*, Copenaghen, 1968

Eroli Giovanni, *Raccolta generale delle iscrizioni pagane esistite ed esistenti nel Pantheon di Roma*, Narni, 1895, con amplissima bibliografia.

Fea Carlo, *Conclusione per l'integrità del Pantheon di M. Agrippa*, ora S. Maria ad Maertyres .. Rome, 1807.

Fea Carlo, *L'integrità del Pantheon rivendicata a M. Agrippa*, Rome, 1820

Forcella Vincenzo, *Iscrizioni delle Chiese e d'altri edifici di Roma dal secolo XI fino ai giorni nostri*, Rome, 1869, I pp.287-310.

Geymuller Henry, *Documents inédits sur les Termes d'Agrippa et le Pantheon*, Lausanne, 1881

Giovannoni Gustavo, *Contributi allo studio delle tecniche delle costruzioni romane*, "Atti del II Congresso nazionale di studi romani", Roma, 1931

Giovannoni Gustavo, *La Cupola di S. Costanza e le volte romane a struttura leggera*, "Atti dal IV Congresso nazionale di studi romani" Roma, 1938

Giovannoni Gustavo, *La tecnica di costruzione presso i Romani*, N.E., Rome 1872.

Giovannoni Gustavo, *Tipi di volte Romane*, Rome, 9/12, 1943.

Hirt Luigi, *Osservazioni istoricco-architettoniche sopra il Pantheon: Bonzi, Camasei, Maioli, Labruzzi*, "Bolettino d'arte, 42,1987,2 pp.91-116

Lugli Giuseppe, *Il Pantheon e i monumenti adiacenti*, Rome, 1962

Lugli Giuseppe, *La tecnica edilizia romana con particolare riguardo a Roma ed il Lazio*, Rome, 1957.

Marta Roberto, *Tecnica costruttiva romana*, 1986

Montini Renzo Umberto, *Tombe dei sovrani in Roma*, Rome 1957, pp.31-37

Nash E. *Pictorial Dictionary of ancient Rome*, London, 1968, II pp. 170-175

36. Santa Maria della Rotonda (G. Lauro, Rome, 1642)